DEPARTMENT OF THE NAVY
HEADQUARTERS UNITED STATES MARINE CORPS
3000 MARINE CORPS PENTAGON
WASHINGTON, D.C. 20350-3000

I0425875

NON-LETHAL WEAPONS (NLW) TRAINING AND READINESS (T&R) MANUAL

DEPARTMENT OF THE NAVY
HEADQUARTERS UNITED STATES MARINE CORPS
3000 MARINE CORPS PENTAGON
WASHINGTON, D.C. 20350-3000

NAVMC 3500.72A
C 469
24 Jan 2012

NAVMC 3500.72A

From: Commandant of the Marine Corps
To: Distribution List

Subj: NON-LETHAL WEAPONS (NLW) TRAINING AND READINESS (T&R) MANUAL

Ref: (a) MCO P3500.72A
      (b) MCO 1553.3A
      (c) MCO 3400.3F
      (d) MCO 3500.27B W/Erratum
      (e) MCRP 3-0A
      (f) MCRP 3-0B
      (g) MCO 1553.2B

1. Purpose. Per reference (a), this T&R Manual establishes training standards, regulations and practices regarding the training of Marines and assigned Navy personnel who will employ NLW. Additionally, it provides tasking for formal schools preparing personnel for NLW employment.

2. Cancellation. NAVMC 3500.72

3. Scope

   a. Per reference (b), commanders will conduct an internal assessment of the unit's ability to execute its mission and develop long-, mid-, and short-range training plans to sustain proficiency and correct deficiencies. Training plans will incorporate these events to standardize training and provide objective assessment of progress toward attaining combat readiness. Commanders will keep records at the unit and individual levels to record training achievements, identify training gaps, and document objective assessments of readiness associated with training Marines. Commanders will use reference (c) to incorporate nuclear, biological, and chemical defense training into training plans and reference (d) to integrate operational risk management. References (e) and (f) provide amplifying information for effective planning and management of training within the unit.

   b. Formal school and training detachment commanders will use references (a) and (g) to ensure programs of instruction meet skill training requirements established in this manual, and provide career-progression training in the events designated for initial training in the formal school environment.

4. Information. Commanding General (CG), Training and Education Command (TECOM) will update this T&R Manual as necessary to provide current and relevant training standards to commanders. All questions pertaining to the

DISTRIBUTION STATEMENT A: Approved for public release; distribution is unlimited.

Marine Corps Ground T&R Program and Unit Training Management should be directed to: CG, TECOM (Ground Training Branch C 469), 1019 Elliot Road, Quantico, VA 22134.

5. <u>Command</u>. This Manual is applicable to the Marine Corps Total Force.

6. <u>Certification</u>. Reviewed and approved this date.

R. C. FOX
By direction

DISTRIBUTION: PCN 10031979300

    Copy to: 7000260 (2)
              8145001 (1)

NAVMC 3500.72A
24 Jan 2012

LOCATOR SHEET

Subj: NON-LETHAL WEAPONS (NLW) TRAINING AND READINESS (T&R) MANUAL

Location: _____
(Indicate location(s) of copy(ies) of this Manual.)

i

RECORD OF CHANGES

Log completed change action as indicated.

Change Number	Date of Change	Date Entered	Signature of Person Incorporated Change

NLW T&R MANUAL

TABLE OF CONTENTS

CHAPTER 1

OVERVIEW

NLW T&R MANUAL

CHAPTER 1

OVERVIEW

1000. INTRODUCTION

1. The T&R Program is the Corps' primary tool for planning, conducting and evaluating training and assessing training readiness. Subject Matter Experts (SMEs) from the operating forces developed core capability Mission Essential Task Lists (METLs) for ground communities derived from the Marine Corps Task List (MCTL). T&R Manuals are built around these METLs and all events contained in T&R Manuals relate directly to this METL. This comprehensive T&R Program will help to ensure the Marine Corps continues to improve its combat readiness by training more efficiently and effectively. Ultimately, this will enhance the Marine Corps' ability to accomplish real-world missions.

2. The T&R Manual contains the individual and collective training requirements to prepare units to accomplish their combat mission. The T&R Manual is not intended to be an encyclopedia that contains every minute detail of how to accomplish training. Instead, it identifies the minimum standards that Marines must be able to perform in combat. The T&R Manual is a fundamental tool for commanders to build and maintain unit combat readiness. Using this tool, leaders can construct and execute an effective training plan that supports the unit's METL. More detailed information on the Marine Corps Ground T&R Program is found in reference (a).

3. The T&R Manual is designed for use by curriculum developers to create courses of instruction and unit commanders to determine predeployment training requirements in preparation for training. This directive focuses on individual and collective tasks performed by OPFOR units and supervised by personnel in the performance of unit Mission Essential Tasks (METs).

1001. UNIT TRAINING

1. The training of Marines to perform as an integrated unit in combat lies at the heart of the T&R program. Unit and individual readiness are directly related. Individual training and the mastery of individual core skills serve as the building blocks for unit combat readiness. A Marine's ability to perform critical skills required in combat is essential. However, it is not necessary to have all individuals within a unit fully trained in order for that organization to accomplish its assigned tasks. Manpower shortfalls, temporary assignments, leave, or other factors outside the commander's control, often affect the ability to conduct individual training. During these periods, unit readiness is enhanced if emphasis is placed on the individual training of Marines on-hand. Subsequently, these Marines will be mission ready and capable of executing as part of a team when the full complement of personnel is available.

2. Commanders will ensure that all tactical training is focused on their combat mission. The T&R Manual is a tool to help develop the unit's training plan. In most cases, unit training should focus on achieving unit proficiency in the core capabilities METL. However, commanders will adjust their training focus to support METLs associated with a major OPLAN/CONPLAN or named operation as designated by their higher commander and reported accordingly in the Defense Readiness Reporting System (DRRS). Tactical training will support the METL in use by the commander and be tailored to meet T&R standards. Commanders at all levels are responsible for effective combat training. The conduct of training in a professional manner consistent with Marine Corps standards cannot be over emphasized.

3. Commanders will provide personnel the opportunity to attend formal and operational level courses of instruction as required by this Manual. Attendance at all formal courses must enhance the warfighting capabilities of the unit as determined by the unit commander.

1002. UNIT TRAINING MANAGEMENT

1. Unit Training Management (UTM) is the application of the Systems Approach to Training (SAT) and the Marine Corps Training Principles. This is accomplished in a manner that maximizes training results and focuses the training priorities of the unit in preparation for the conduct of its wartime mission.

2. UTM techniques, described in references (b) and (e), provide commanders with the requisite tools and techniques to analyze, design, develop, implement, and evaluate the training of their unit. The Marine Corps Training Principles, explained in reference (b), provide sound and proven direction and are flexible enough to accommodate the demands of local conditions. These principles are not inclusive, nor do they guarantee success. They are guides that commanders can use to manage unit-training programs. The Marine Corps training principles are:

- Train as you fight
- Make commanders responsible for training
- Use standards-based training
- Use performance-oriented training
- Use mission-oriented training
- Train the MAGTF to fight as a combined arms team
- Train to sustain proficiency
- Train to challenge

3. To maintain an efficient and effective training program, leaders at every level must understand and implement UTM. Guidance for UTM and the process for establishing effective programs are contained in references (a) through (g).

1003. SUSTAINMENT AND EVALUATION OF TRAINING

1. The evaluation of training is necessary to properly prepare Marines for combat. Evaluations are either formal or informal, and performed by members

of the unit (internal evaluation) or from an external command (external
evaluation).

2. Marines are expected to maintain proficiency in the training events for
their MOS at the appropriate grade or billet to which assigned. Leaders are
responsible for recording the training achievements of their Marines.
Whether it involves individual or collective training events, they must
ensure proficiency is sustained by requiring retraining of each event at or
before expiration of the designated sustainment interval. Performance of the
training event, however, is not sufficient to ensure combat readiness.
Leaders at all levels must evaluate the performance of their Marines and the
unit as they complete training events, and only record successful
accomplishment of training based upon the evaluation. The goal of evaluation
is to ensure that correct methods are employed to achieve the desired
standard, or the Marines understand how they need to improve in order to
attain the standard. Leaders must determine whether credit for completing a
training event is recorded if the standard was not achieved. While
successful accomplishment is desired, debriefing of errors can result in
successful learning that will allow ethical recording of training event
completion. Evaluation is a continuous process that is integral to training
management and is conducted by leaders at every level and during all phases
of planning and the conduct of training. To ensure training is efficient and
effective, evaluation is an integral part of the training plan. Ultimately,
leaders remain responsible for determining if the training was effective.

3. The purpose of formal and informal evaluation is to provide commanders
with a process to determine a unit's/Marine's proficiency in the tasks that
must be performed in combat. Informal evaluations are conducted during every
training evolution. Formal evaluations are often scenario-based, focused on
the unit's METs, based on collective training standards, and usually
conducted during higher-level collective events. References (a) and (f)
provide further guidance on the conduct of informal and formal evaluations
using the Marine Corps Ground T&R Program.

1004. ORGANIZATION

1. T&R Manuals are organized in one of two methods: unit-based or
community-based. Unit-based T&R Manuals are written to support a type of
unit (Infantry, Artillery, Tanks, etc.) and contain both collective and
individual training standards. Community-based are written to support an
Occupational Field, a group of related Military Occupational Specialties
(MOSs), or billets within an organization (EOD, NBC, Intel, etc.), and can
contain both collective and individual training standards. T&R Manuals are
comprised of chapters that contain unit METs, collective training standards
(CTS), and individual training standards (ITS) for each MOS, billet, etc.

1005. T&R EVENT CODING

1. T&R events are coded for ease of reference. Each event has up-to a 4-4-
4-digit identifier. The first up-to four digits are referred to as a
"community" and represent the unit type or occupation. The second up-to four
digits represent the functional or duty area. The last four digits represent
the level and sequence of the event.

2. The T&R levels are illustrated in Figure 1. An example of the T&R coding used in this Manual is shown in Figure 2.

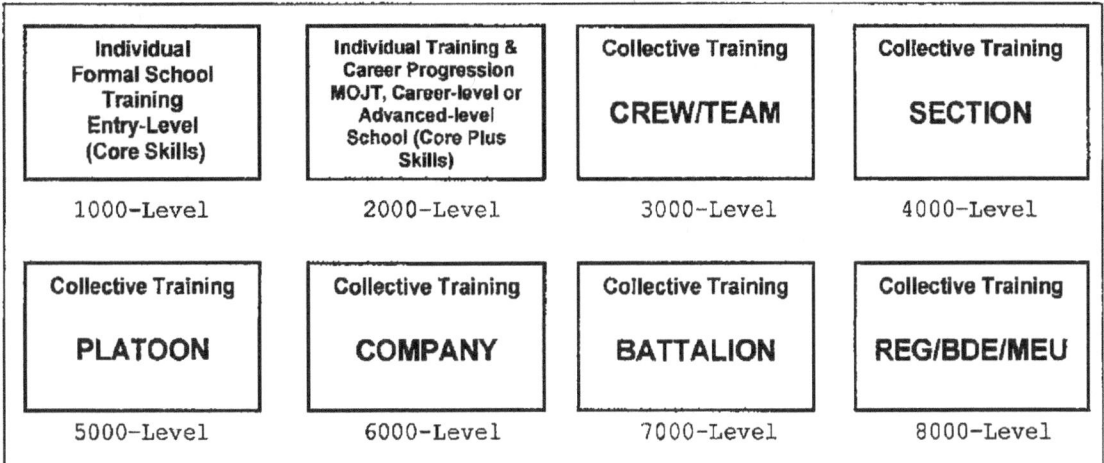

Figure 1: T&R Event Levels

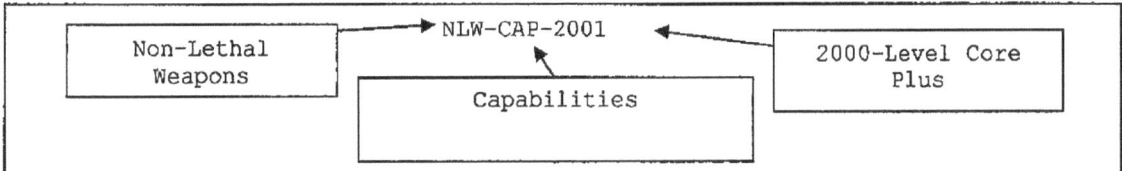

Figure 2: T&R Event Coding

1006. COMBAT READINESS PERCENTAGE

1. The Marine Corps Ground T&R Program includes processes to assess readiness of units and individual Marines. Every unit in the Marine Corps maintains a basic level of readiness based on the training and experience of the Marines in the unit. Even units that never trained together are capable of accomplishing some portion of their missions. Combat readiness assessment does not associate a quantitative value for this baseline of readiness, but uses a "Combat Readiness Percentage", as a method to provide a concise descriptor of the recent training accomplishments of units and Marines.

2. Combat Readiness Percentage (CRP) is the percentage of required training events that a unit or Marine accomplishes within specified sustainment intervals.

3. In unit-based T&R Manuals, unit combat readiness is assessed as a percentage of the successfully completed and current (within sustainment interval) key training events called "Evaluation-Coded" (E-Coded) events. E-Coded events and unit CRP calculation are described in follow-on paragraphs. CRP achieved through the completion of E-Coded events is directly relevant to readiness assessment in DRRS.

4. Individual combat readiness, in both unit-based and community-based T&R Manuals, is assessed as the percentage of required individual events in which a Marine is current. This translates as the percentage of training events for his/her MOS and grade (or billet) that the Marine successfully completes within the directed sustainment interval. Individual skills are developed through a combination of 1000-level training (entry-level formal school courses), individual on-the-job training in 2000-level events, and follow-on formal school training. Skill proficiency is maintained by retraining in each event per the specified sustainment interval.

1007. EVALUATION-CODED (E-CODED) EVENTS

1. Unit-type T&R Manuals can contain numerous unit events, some for the whole unit and others for integral parts that serve as building blocks for training. To simplify training management and readiness assessment, only collective events that are critical components of a mission essential task (MET), or key indicators of a unit's readiness, are used to generate CRP for a MET. These critical or key events are designated in the T&R Manual as Evaluation-Coded (E-Coded) events. Formal evaluation of unit performance in these events is recommended because of their value in assessing combat readiness. Only E-Coded events are used to calculate CRP for each MET.

2. The use of a METL-based training program allows the commander discretion in training. This makes the T&R Manual a training tool rather than a prescriptive checklist.

1008. CRP CALCULATION

1. Collective training begins at the 3000 level (team, crew or equivalent). Unit training plans are designed to accomplish the events that support the unit METL while simultaneously sustaining proficiency in individual core skills. Using the battalion-based (unit) model, the battalion (7000-level) has collective events that directly support a MET on the METL. These collective events are E-Coded and the only events that contribute to unit CRP. This is done to assist commanders in prioritizing the training toward the METL, taking into account resource, time, and personnel constraints.

2. Unit CRP increases after the completion of E-Coded events. The number of E-Coded events for the MET determines the value of each E-Coded event. For example, if there are 4 E-Coded events for a MET, each is worth 25% of MET CRP. MET CRP is calculated by adding the percentage of each completed and current (within sustainment interval) E-Coded training event. The percentage for each MET is calculated the same way and all are added together and divided by the number of METS to determine unit CRP. For ease of calculation, we will say that each MET has 4 E-Coded events, each contributing 25% towards the completion of the MET. If the unit has completed and is current on three of the four E-Coded events for a given MET, then they have completed 75% of the MET. The CRP for each MET is added together and divided by the number of METS to get unit CRP; unit CRP is the average of MET CRP.

For Example:

```
MET 1:  75% complete  (3 of 4 E-Coded events trained)
MET 2:  100% complete (6 of 6 E-Coded events trained)
MET 3:  25% complete  (1 of 4 E-Coded events trained)
MET 4:  50% complete  (2 of 4 E-Coded events trained)
MET 5:  75% complete  (3 of 4 E-Coded events trained)
```

To get unit CRP, simply add the CRP for each MET and divide by the number of METS:

MET CRP: 75 + 100 + 25 + 50 + 75 = 325

Unit CRP: 325 (total MET CRP)/5 (total number of METS) = 65%

1009. T&R EVENT COMPOSITION

1. This section explains each of the components of a T&R event. These items are included in all events in each T&R Manual.

   a. Event Code (see Sect 1006). The event code is a 4-4-4 character set. For individual training events, the first 4 characters indicate the occupational function. The second 4 characters indicate functional area (TAC, CBTS, VOPS, etc.). The third 4 characters are simply a numerical designator for the event.

   b. Event Title. The event title is the name of the event.

   c. E-Coded. This is a "yes/no" category to indicate whether or not the event is E-Coded. If yes, the event contributes toward the CRP of the associated MET. The value of each E-Coded event is based on number of E-Coded events for that MET. Refer to paragraph 1008 for detailed explanation of E-Coded events.

   d. Supported MET(s). List all METs that are supported by the training event.

   e. Sustainment Interval. This is the period, expressed in number of months, between evaluation or retraining requirements. Skills and capabilities acquired through the accomplishment of training events are refreshed at pre-determined intervals. It is essential that these intervals are adhered to in order to ensure Marines maintain proficiency.

   f. Billet. Individual training events may contain a list of billets within the community that are responsible for performing that event. This ensures that the billets expected tasks are clearly articulated and a Marine's readiness to perform in that billet is measured.

   g. Grade. Each individual training event will list the rank(s) at which Marines are required to learn and sustain the training event.

   h. Initial Training Setting. For Individual T&R Events only, this specifies the location for initial instruction of the training event in one of three categories (formal school, managed on-the-job training, distance learning). Regardless of the specified Initial Training Setting, any T&R event may be introduced and evaluated during managed on-the-job training.

(1) "FORMAL" - When the Initial Training Setting of an event is identified as "FORMAL" (formal school), the appropriate formal school or training detachment is required to provide initial training in the event. Conversely, formal schools and training detachments are not authorized to provide training in events designated as Initial Training Setting "MOJT" or "DL." Since the duration of formal school training must be constrained to optimize Operating Forces' manning, this element provides the mechanism for Operating Forces' prioritization of training requirements for both entry-level (1000-level) and career-level (2000-level) T&R Events. For formal schools and training detachments, this element defines the requirements for content of courses.

(2) "DL" - Identifies the training event as a candidate for initial training via a Distance Learning product (correspondence course or MarineNet course).

(3) "MOJT" - Events specified for Managed On-the-Job Training are to be introduced to Marines, and evaluated, as part of training within a unit by supervisory personnel.

i. Event Description. Provide a description of the event purpose, objectives, goals, and requirements. It is a general description of an action requiring learned skills and knowledge (e.g. Camouflage the M1A1 Tank).

j. Condition. Describe the condition(s), under which tasks are performed. Conditions are based on a "real world" operational environment. They indicate what is provided (equipment, materials, manuals, aids, etc.), environmental constraints, conditions under which the task is performed, and any specific cues or indicators to which the performer must respond. When resources or safety requirements limit the conditions, this is stated.

k. Standard. The standard indicates the basis for judging effectiveness of the performance. It consists of a carefully worded statement that identifies the proficiency level expected when the task is performed. The standard provides the minimum acceptable performance parameters and is strictly adhered to. The standard for collective events is general, describing the desired end-state or purpose of the event. While the standard for individual events specifically describe to what proficiency level in terms of accuracy, speed, sequencing, quality of performance, adherence to procedural guidelines, etc., the event is accomplished.

l. Event Components. Describe the actions composing the event and help the user determine what must be accomplished and to properly plan for the event.

m. Prerequisite Events. Prerequisites are academic training or other T&R events that must be completed prior to attempting the task. They are lower-level events or tasks that give the individual/unit the skills required to accomplish the event. They can also be planning steps, administrative requirements, or specific parameters that build toward mission accomplishment.

n. Chained Events. Collective T&R events are supported by lower-level collective and individual T&R events. This enables unit leaders to effectively identify subordinate T&R events that ultimately support specific mission essential tasks. When the accomplishment of any upper-level events, by their nature, result in the performance of certain subordinate and related events, the events are "chained." The completion of chained events will update sustainment interval credit (and CRP for E-Coded events) for the related subordinate level events.

o. Related Events. Provide a list of all Individual Training Standards that support the event.

p. References. The training references are utilized to determine task performance steps, grading criteria, and ensure standardization of training procedures. They assist the trainee in satisfying the performance standards, or the trainer in evaluating the effectiveness of task completion. References are also important to the development of detailed training plans.

q. Distance Learning Products (IMI, CBT, MCI, etc.). Include this component when the event can be taught via one of these media methods vice attending a formal course of instruction or receiving MOJT.

r. Support Requirements. This is a list of the external and internal support the unit and Marines will need to complete the event. The list includes, but is not limited to:

- Range(s)/Training Area
- Ordnance
- Equipment
- Materials
- Other Units/Personnel
- Other Support Requirements

s. Miscellaneous. Provide any additional information that assists in the planning and execution of the event. Miscellaneous information may include, but is not limited to:

- Admin Instructions
- Special Personnel Certifications
- Equipment Operating Hours
- Road Miles

2. Community-based T&R Manuals have several additional components not found in unit-based T&R Manuals. These additions do not apply to this T&R Manual.

1010. CBRN TRAINING

1. All personnel assigned to the operating force must be trained in chemical, biological, radiological, and nuclear defense (CBRN), in order to survive and continue their mission in this environment. Individual proficiency standards are defined as survival and basic operating standards. Survival standards are those that the individual must master in order to survive CBRN attacks. Basic operating standards are those that the

individual, and collectively the unit, must perform to continue operations in a CBRN environment.

2. In order to develop and maintain the ability to operate in a CBRN environment, CBRN training is an integral part of the training plan and events in this T&R Manual. Units should train under CBRN conditions whenever possible. Per reference (c), all units must be capable of accomplishing their assigned mission in a contaminated environment.

1011. NIGHT TRAINING

1. While it is understood that all personnel and units of the operating force are capable of performing their assigned mission in "every climate and place," current doctrine emphasizes the requirement to perform assigned missions at night and during periods of limited visibility. Basic skills are significantly more difficult when visibility is limited.

2. To ensure units are capable of accomplishing their mission they must train under the conditions of limited visibility. Units should strive to conduct all events in this T&R Manual during both day and night/limited visibility conditions. When there is limited training time available, night training should take precedence over daylight training, contingent on individual, crew, and unit proficiency.

1012. OPERATIONAL RISK MANAGEMENT (ORM)

1. ORM is a process that enables commanders to plan for and minimize risk while still accomplishing the mission. It is a decision making tool used by Marines at all levels to increase operational effectiveness by anticipating hazards and reducing the potential for loss, thereby increasing the probability of a successful mission. ORM minimizes risks to acceptable levels, commensurate with mission accomplishment.

2. Commanders, leaders, maintainers, planners, and schedulers will integrate risk assessment in the decision-making process and implement hazard controls to reduce risk to acceptable levels. Applying the ORM process will reduce mishaps, lower costs, and provide for more efficient use of resources. ORM assists the commander in conserving lives and resources and avoiding unnecessary risk, making an informed decision to implement a course of action (COA), identifying feasible and effective control measures where specific measures do not exist, and providing reasonable alternatives for mission accomplishment. Most importantly, ORM assists the commander in determining the balance between training realism and unnecessary risks in training, the impact of training operations on the environment, and the adjustment of training plans to fit the level of proficiency and experience of Sailors/Marines and leaders. Further guidance for ORM is found in references (b) and (d).

1013. APPLICATION OF SIMULATION

1. Simulations/Simulators and other training devices shall be used when they are capable of effectively and economically supplementing training on the

identified training task. Particular emphasis shall be placed on simulators
that provide training that might be limited by safety considerations or
constraints on training space, time, or other resources. When deciding on
simulation issues, the primary consideration shall be improving the quality
of training and consequently the state of readiness. Potential savings in
operating and support costs normally shall be an important secondary
consideration.

2. Each training event contains information relating to the applicability of
simulation. If simulator training applies to the event, then the applicable
simulator(s) is/are listed in the "Simulation" section and the CRP for
simulation training is given. This simulation training can either be used in
place of live training, at the reduced CRP indicated; or can be used as a
precursor training for the live event, i.e., weapons simulators, convoy
trainers, observed fire trainers, etc. It is recommended that tasks be
performed by simulation prior to being performed in a live-fire environment.
However, in the case where simulation is used as a precursor for the live
event, then the unit will receive credit for the live event CRP only. If a
tactical situation develops that precludes performing the live event, the
unit would then receive credit for the simulation CRP.

1014. MARINE CORPS GROUND T&R PROGRAM

1. The Marine Corps Ground T&R Program continues to evolve. The vision for
Ground T&R Program is to publish a T&R Manual for every readiness-reporting
unit so that core capability METs are clearly defined with supporting
collective training standards, and to publish community-based T&R Manuals for
all occupational fields whose personnel augment other units to increase their
combat and/or logistic capabilities. The vision for this program includes
plans to provide a Marine Corps training management information system that
enables tracking of unit and individual training accomplishments by unit
commanders and small unit leaders, automatically computing CRP for both units
and individual Marines based upon MOS and rank (or billet). Linkage of T&R
Events to the Marine Corps Task List (MCTL), through the core capability
METs, has enabled objective assessment of training readiness in the DRRS.

2. DRRS measures and reports on the readiness of military forces and the
supporting infrastructure to meet missions and goals assigned by the
Secretary of Defense. With unit CRP based on the unit's training toward its
METs, the CRP will provide a more accurate picture of a unit's readiness.
This will give fidelity to future funding requests and factor into the
allocation of resources. Additionally, the Ground T&R Program will help to
ensure training remains focused on mission accomplishment and that training
readiness reporting is tied to units' METLs.

CHAPTER 2

MISSION ESSENTIAL TASKS MATRIX

The Recruiting and Retention T&R Manual does not contain a Mission
Essential Task Matrix as there are no Recruiting and Retention units which
report readiness in the Defense Readiness Reporting System (DRRS). Although
the collective and individual events contained in this manual are not
directly linked to Mission Essential Tasks, they directly support the Marine
Corps ability to meet the capabilities identified in the Marine Corps Task
List (MCO 3500.26_).

NLW T&R MANUAL

CHAPTER 3

COLLECTIVE EVENTS

CHAPTER 3

COLLECTIVE EVENTS

3000. PURPOSE. This chapter includes all collective events for the employment of non-lethal weapons. Each collective event is composed of component events that provide the major actions required. This may be likely actions, list of functions, or procedures. Accomplishment and proficiency level required of component events are determined by the event standard.

3001. EVENT CODING. Events in the T&R Manual are depicted with an up to 12-digit, 3-field alphanumeric system, i.e. XXXX-XXXX-XXXX. In some cases, all 12 digits may not be used. This chapter utilizes the following methodology:

   a. Field one - Each event starts with "NLW" indicating that the event is for Non-Lethal Weapons.

   b. Field two - This field is alpha characters indicating a functional area.

      CRWD - Crowd Control

   c. Field three - This field provides the unit level at which the event is accomplished and numerical sequencing.

3002. INDEX OF COLLECTIVE EVENTS

Event Code	E-Coded	Event	Page
3000-Level			
NLW-CRWD-3001		Execute crowd control formations	3-4
NLW-CRWD-3002		Execute crowd control tactics	3-4
NLW-CRWD-3003		Emplace non-lethal devices	3-5

3003. 3000-LEVEL EVENTS

NLW-CRWD-3001: Execute crowd control formations

SUPPORTED MET(S): None

EVALUATION-CODED: NO   SUSTAINMENT INTERVAL: 12 months

CONDITION: Given a mission, EOFMM and personnel.

STANDARD: In order to manage and neutralize changes/escalations in crowd behavior.

EVENT COMPONENTS:
1. Perform the column formation.
2. Perform the on-line formation.
3. Perform the echelon formation.
4. Perform the wedge formation.
5. Perform open formations.
6. Redeploy a civil disturbance unit, if required.
7. Access the situation.
8. Deploy a civil disturbance unit.

REFERENCES:
1. FM 3-19.15 Civil Disturbance Operations
2. MCWP 3-15.8 Multi-service Procedures for the Tactical Employment of Non-lethal Weapons

SUPPORT REQUIREMENTS:

   EQUIPMENT: Marine Corps Escalation of Force Mission Module (EOFMM)

NLW-CRWD-3002: Execute crowd control tactics

SUPPORTED MET(S): None

EVALUATION-CODED: NO   SUSTAINMENT INTERVAL: 12 months

CONDITION: Given a mission, EOFMM and personnel.

STANDARD: In order to manage and neutralize changes/escalations in crowd behavior.

EVENT COMPONENTS:
1. Conduct clearance team operation, if required.
2. Conduct extraction team operation, if required.

PREREQUISITE EVENTS: NLW-CRWD-3001

REFERENCES:
1. FM 3-19.15 Civil Disturbance Operations

2. MARADMIN 560/08 Training and Use of Human Electro-Muscular Incapacitation (HEMI) Devices
3. MCO 5500.6F Arming of Law Enforcement and Security Personnel and the Use of Deadly Force
4. MCWP 3-15.8 Multi-service Procedures for the Tactical Employment of Non-lethal Weapons
5. NLW Manual Controlled F.O.R.C.E. Manual for Mechanical Advantage Control Holds

SUPPORT REQUIREMENTS:

ORDNANCE:

DODIC	Quantity
AA29 Cartridge, 12 Gauge Non-Lethal Bean	10 rounds per Team
AA30 Cartridge, 12 Gauge Launching Cup fo	2 cartridges per Team
AA31 12GA Cartridge, Fin Stabilized Nonle	10 rounds per Team
AB08 1310-01-536-1536 12 Ga. Extended Ran	10 rounds per Team
BA07 Cartridge, 40mm Foam Rubber Baton No	10 rounds per Team
BA08 40MM Cartridge, Rubber Ball Non-lethal	10 rounds per Team
G874 Fuze, Hand Grenade M201A1/M201A1-1	4 fuses per Team
GG04 Grenade, Rubber Ball Non-Lethal 9590	4 grenades per Team
GG09 Grenade M84, Stun/Diversionary Flash	2 grenades per Team
GG13- Grenade, Practice Body Non-Lethal	4 grenades per Team
GG20- Grenade, Hand Stun	2 grenades per Team

EQUIPMENT: Marine Corps Escalation of Force Mission Module (EOFMM) and X26E TASER (NSN 1095015432189), Cartridge-25FT XP (NSN 1095015331733)

OTHER SUPPORT REQUIREMENTS: These are additional DODICs supported at the INIWIC course. These are USA DODICs: (12ga AA51, AA52, LA51, LA52) (40mm BA06, BA13, BA24, BA25, BA26, BA27),(66 mm FZ15,) , (WA97 MCCM nonlethal claymore) FN303 compressed air launcher, FN303 training rounds, FN303 Airbank, FN303 airbottles

---

NLW-CRWD-3003: Emplace non-lethal devices

SUPPORTED MET(S): None

EVALUATION-CODED: NO   SUSTAINMENT INTERVAL: 12 months

CONDITION: Given a mission and personnel.

STANDARD: In order to enhance force protection efforts.

EVENT COMPONENTS:
1. Access the situation.
2. Determine appropriate device.
3. Employ selected device.
4. Assess effects on target.
5. Reengage target, if applicable.
6. Recover equipment, as required.

PREREQUISITE EVENTS: NLW-CRWD-3001

REFERENCES:
1. 0000V Rev00 Magnum Spike 2000, Phoenix International
2. FM 3-19.15 Civil Disturbance Operations
3. MCWP 3-15.8 Multi-service Procedures for the Tactical Employment of Non-lethal Weapons
4. MRAD Manual Rev A American Technology Corp Medium Acoustic Device Manual
5. SC0001 Rev00 Sound Commander Operations and Maintenance Manual
6. TM 5-4240-536-10 Barrier, Vehicle Arresting, Portable: Vehicle Lightweight Arresting Device (VLAD), M@
7. TM 9-1377-617-12 Munitions, Crowd Control Modular, Nonlethal: M5
8. TM 9-6350-382-12 Barrier, Vehicle Arresting, Portable (PVAB), M1

SUPPORT REQUIREMENTS:

ORDNANCE:

DODIC	Quantity
AA29 Cartridge, 12 Gauge Non-Lethal Bean	10
AA30 Cartridge, 12 Gauge Launching Cup fo	5
AA31 12GA Cartridge, Fin Stabilized Nonle	10
BA07 Cartridge, 40mm Foam Rubber Baton No	10
BA09 Cartridge, 40mm Wooden Baton Non-Let	10
GG04 Grenade, Rubber Ball Non-Lethal 9590	2

EQUIPMENT: Marine Corps Escalation force mission module

OTHER SUPPORT REQUIREMENTS: The Army DODIC for the Modular Crowd Control Munition (WA97) is part of INIWIC's munitions.

NLW T&R MANUAL

CHAPTER 4

INDIVIDUAL EVENTS

CHAPTER 4

INDIVIDUAL EVENTS

4000. PURPOSE. This chapter details the individual user events required for the Non-Lethal Weapons (NLW) Program. Each individual event contained in this chapter provides an event title, along with the conditions events will be performed under, and the standard to which the event must be performed to be successful.

4001. EVENT CODING. Events in the T&R Manual are depicted with a 12 field alphanumeric system, i.e. NLW-CAP-2001. This chapter utilizes the following methodology:

　　a.　Field one - Each event starts with "NLW" indicating that the event is for Non-Lethal Weapons.

　　b.　Field two - This field is alpha characters indicating a functional area.

　　　　CAP　- Capabilities
　　　　INST - Instructor
　　　　TECH - Techniques
　　　　WPNS - Weapons

　　c.　Field three - This field provides event level and numerical sequencing. This chapter contains the following event levels:

　　　2000 - Core plus skills

4002. INDEX OF INDIVIDUAL EVENTS

4003. 2000-LEVEL EVENTS

NLW-TECH-2001: Employ civil disturbance techniques

EVALUATION-CODED: NO　　　　**SUSTAINMENT INTERVAL**: 12 months

GRADES: PVT, PFC, LCPL, CPL, SGT, SSGT, GYSGT, MSGT, 2NDLT, 1STLT, CAPT

INITIAL TRAINING SETTING: MOJT

CONDITION: Given a mission, EOFMM and NL weapon/munitions.

STANDARD: In order to determine, manage, and neutralize changes/escalation in crowd behavior.

PERFORMANCE STEPS:
1. Identify characteristics of a crowd.
2. Perform a civil disturbance formation(s).
3. Conduct over watch when required.
4. Perform clearance operations when applicable.
5. Perform extraction operations when applicable.
6. Employ non- lethal weapons/capabilities when applicable.

REFERENCES:
1: FM 3-19.15 Civil Disturbance Operations
2. MCWP 3-15.8 Multi-service Procedures for the Tactical Employment of Non-lethal Weapons
3. NLW Manual Controlled F.O.R.C.E. Manual for Mechanical Advantage Control Holds

SUPPORT REQUIREMENTS:

　ORDNANCE:

DODIC	Quantity
AA29 Cartridge, 12 Gauge Non-Lethal Bean	5 rounds per Marine
AA30 Cartridge, 12 Gauge Launching Cup fo	1 round per Marine
AA31 12GA Cartridge, Fin Stabilized Nonle	5 rounds per Marine
AB08 1310-01-536-1536 12 Ga. Extended Ran	5 rounds per Marine
BA07 Cartridge, 40mm Foam Rubber Baton No	5 rounds per Marine
BA08 40MM Cartridge, Rubber Ball Nonlethal	5 rounds per Marine
G874 Fuze, Hand Grenade M201A1/M201A1-1	2 fuses per Marine
GG04 Grenade, Rubber Ball Non-Lethal 9590	1 grenades per Marine
GG05 Grenade, Practice Body Non-Lethal	2 grenades per Marine
GG09 Grenade M84, Stun/Diversionary Flash	1 grenades per Marine
GG13 Grenade, Practice Body Non-Lethal	2 grenades per Marine
GG20 Grenade, Hand Stun	1 grenades per Marine

EQUIPMENT: X26E TASER (NSN 1095015432189), Cartridge-25FT XP (NSN 1095015331733), Escalation of Force Mission Module (EOFMM)

OTHER SUPPORT REQUIREMENTS: These are additional DODICs supported at the INIWIC course. These are USA DODICs: (12ga AA51, AA52, LA51, LA52) (40mm BA06, BA13, BA24, BA25, BA26, BA27),(66 mm FZ15,) , (WA97 MCCM nonlethal claymore)Long Range Acoustic Device (LRAD)

NLW-TECH-2002: Employ Close Range Subject Control (CRSC) techniques

EVALUATION-CODED: NO   **SUSTAINMENT INTERVAL:** 12 months

GRADES: PVT, PFC, LCPL, CPL, SGT, SSGT, GYSGT, MSGT, 2NDLT, 1STLT, CAPT

INITIAL TRAINING SETTING: MOJT

CONDITION: Given a mission, EOFMM and NL weapon/munitions.

STANDARD: In order to control a subject while preventing injury to yourself and others.

PERFORMANCE STEPS:
1. Access situation.
2. Determine appropriate control procedure.
3. Utilize straight/expandable baton if applicable.
4. Execute procedure(s).

REFERENCES:
1. MCWP 3-15.8 Multi-service Procedures for the Tactical Employment of Non-lethal Weapons
2. NLW Force continuum diagram
3. NLW Manual Controlled F.O.R.C.E. Manual for Mechanical Advantage Control Holds
4. Non-lethal MANADNOCK Baton Strike Chart

SUPPORT REQUIREMENTS:

  EQUIPMENT: Marine Corps Escalation of Force Mission Module (EOFMM)

NLW-TECH-2003: Employ Close Range Subject Control (CRSC) takedown techniques

EVALUATION-CODED: NO   **SUSTAINMENT INTERVAL:** 12 months

GRADES: PVT, PFC, LCPL, CPL, SGT, SSGT, GYSGT, 2NDLT, 1STLT, CAPT

INITIAL TRAINING SETTING: MOJT

CONDITION: Given a mission, EOFMM and NL weapon/munitions.

STANDARD: In order to control a subject, while preventing injury to yourself and others.

PERFORMANCE STEPS:
1. Access situation.
2. Determine appropriate control procedure.
3. Execute procedure(s).
4. Apply restraints as required.

PREREQUISITE EVENTS: NLW-TECH-2002

REFERENCES:
1. MCWP 3-15.8 Multi-service Procedures for the Tactical Employment of Non-lethal Weapons
2. NLW Force continuum diagram
3. NLW Manual Controlled F.O.R.C.E. Manual for Mechanical Advantage Control Holds
4. Non-lethal MANADNOCK Baton Strike Chart

SUPPORT REQUIREMENTS:

   EQUIPMENT: Marine Corps Escalation of Force Mission Module (EOFMM)

NLW-CAP-2101: Employ non-lethal devices

EVALUATION-CODED: NO   SUSTAINMENT INTERVAL: 12 months

DESCRIPTION: Non-lethal devices encompass but are not limited to the following: Ocular Hail and Warning Device (OHWD), Acoustic Hailing Device (AHD), Vehicle Arresting/Stopping Device(s), Oleoresin Capsicum (OC), and Human Electro-Muscular Incapacitation (HEMI) device.

GRADES: PVT, PFC, LCPL, CPL, SGT, SSGT, GYSGT, MSGT, 2NDLT, 1STLT, CAPT

INITIAL TRAINING SETTING: MOJT

CONDITION: Given a mission.

STANDARD: In order to halt or deter a vehicle, group, or individual.

PERFORMANCE STEPS:
1. Conduct PMCS.
2. Determine appropriate device.
3. Install on weapon platform, if required.
4. Emplace device, if applicable.
5. Engage target, if applicable.
6. Assess effects on target.
7. Utilize restraining devices, if required.

REFERENCES:
1. 0000V Rev00 Magnum Spike 2000, Phoenix International
2. B.E. Myers 532-M Operator's Manual "Glare" Minigreen Laser System
3. B.E. Myers GBDIIIC Laser Operator's Manual for GBDIIIC
4. MARADMIN 560/08 Training and Use of Human Electro-Muscular Incapacitation (HEMI) Devices
5. MCWP 3-15.8 Multi-service Procedures for the Tactical Employment of Non-lethal Weapons
6. MRAD Manual Rev A American Technology Corp Medium Acoustic Device Manual
7. SC0001 Rev00 Sound Commander Operations and Maintenance Manual
8. TM 5-4240-536-10 Barrier, Vehicle Arresting, Portable: Vehicle Lightweight Arresting Device (VLAD), M@
9. TM 9-6350-382-12 Barrier, Vehicle Arresting, Portable (PVAB), M1

SUPPORT REQUIREMENTS:

  EQUIPMENT: LA9P non lethal laser system, Laser eye protection, X26 HEMI device, 25xp taser cartridge

  OTHER SUPPORT REQUIREMENTS: Marine Corps Escalation of Force Mission Module (EOFMM)

NLW-WPNS-2201: Employ non-lethal munitions

EVALUATION-CODED: NO   SUSTAINMENT INTERVAL: 12 months

DESCRIPTION: Ammunition requirements encompass but are not limited to the following non-lethal single/multiple projectile munitions: 12 gauge, 40mm, 66mm and hand thrown diversion and/or warning.

GRADES: PVT, PFC, LCPL, CPL, SGT, SSGT, GYSGT, MSGT, 2NDLT, 1STLT, CAPT

INITIAL TRAINING SETTING: MOJT

CONDITION: Given a mission, PPE and NL capable weapons platform.

STANDARD: Ensuring rounds strike a subject in an appropriate target area of the body.

PERFORMANCE STEPS:
1. Assess situation.
2. Determine appropriate munitions.
3. Engage targets.
4. Assess desired effects on target.

REFERENCES:
1. CJCSI 3121.01B Chairman of the Joint Chiefs of Staff Instruction, Standing Rules of Engagement/Standing Rules for the Use of Force for US Forces
2. FN 303 OP Manual FN303 Less Lethal Launcher Operator Manual, May 2002
3. MCO 5500.6F Arming of Law Enforcement and Security Personnel and the Use of Deadly Force
4. MCWP 3-15.8 Multi-service Procedures for the Tactical Employment of Non-lethal Weapons
5. NLW Force continuum diagram
6. Non-lethal MANADNOCK Baton Strike Chart

SUPPORT REQUIREMENTS:

  ORDNANCE:

DODIC	Quantity
AA29 Cartridge, 12 Gauge Non-Lethal Bean	5 rounds per Marine
AA30 Cartridge, 12 Gauge Launching Cup fo	1 cartridges per Marine
AA31 12GA Cartridge, Fin Stabilized Nonle	5 rounds per Marine
AB08 1310-01-536-1536 12 Ga. Extended Ran	5 rounds per Marine
BA07 Cartridge, 40mm Foam Rubber Baton No	5 rounds per Marine
BA08 40MM Cartridge, Rubber Ball Nonlethal	5 rounds per Marine
G874 Fuze, Hand Grenade M201A1/M201A1-1	2 fuses per Marine

```
GG04 Grenade, Rubber Ball Non-Lethal 9590    2 grenades per Marine
GG09 Grenade M84, Stun/Diversionary Flash    1 grenades per Marine
GG13 Grenade, Practice Body Non-Lethal       2 grenades per Marine
GG20 Grenade, Hand Stun                       1 grenades per Marine
```

EQUIPMENT: Marine Corps Escalation of Force Mission Module (EOFMM)

OTHER SUPPORT REQUIREMENTS: These are additional DODICs supported at the INIWIC course. These are USA DODICs: (12ga AA51, AA52, LA51, LA52) (40mm BA06, BA13, BA24, BA25, BA26, BA27), (66 mm FZ15,), (WA97 MCCM nonlethal claymore), FN303 compressed air launcher and FN303 airbank, FN303 airbottles, FN303 projectiles

---

NLW-INST-2501: Conduct Non-lethal Capabilities Training

EVALUATION-CODED: NO   **SUSTAINMENT INTERVAL:** 24 months

BILLETS: Non-Lethal Weapons Instructor

GRADES: CPL, SGT, SSGT, GYSGT, MSGT, 2NDLT, 1STLT, CAPT

INITIAL TRAINING SETTING: FORMAL

CONDITION: Given curriculum materials, personnel to be trained, PPE, EOFMM and an instructional setting.

STANDARD: In order to ensure personnel are trained on the proper employment of NLW, as well as their capabilities and limitation.

PERFORMANCE STEPS:
1. Train employment of NL capabilities.
2. Train employment of NL techniques.
3. Train the employment of NL weapons/munitions.
4. Maintain administrative reports.

REFERENCES:
1. MCWP 3-15.8 Multi-service Procedures for the Tactical Employment of Non-lethal Weapons
2. SAT MANUAL Systems Approach to Training Manual

SUPPORT REQUIREMENTS:

  ORDNANCE:

DODIC	Quantity
AA29 Cartridge, 12 Gauge Non-Lethal Bean	5 rounds per Marine
AA30 Cartridge, 12 Gauge Launching Cup fo	2 round per Marine
AA31 12GA Cartridge, Fin Stabilized Nonle	5 rounds per Marine
AB08 1310-01-536-1536 12 Ga. Extended Ran	5 rounds per Marine
BA07 Cartridge, 40mm Foam Rubber Baton No	5 rounds per Marine
BA08 40MM Cartridge, Rubber Ball Nonletha	5 rounds per Marine
G874 Fuze, Hand Grenade M201A1/M201A1-1	2 fuses per Marine
GG04 Grenade, Rubber Ball Non-Lethal 9590	2 grenades per Marine
GG09 Grenade M84, Stun/Diversionary Flash	1 grenades per Marine

GG13 Grenade, Practice Body Non-Lethal   2 grenades per Marine
GG20 Grenade, Hand Stun   1 grenades per Platoon

EQUIPMENT: Marine Corps Escalation of Force Mission Module (EOFMM), X26 HEMI device, 25XP taser cartridge, LA9P nonlethal laser system

OTHER SUPPORT REQUIREMENTS: These are additional DODICs consumed at the INIWIC course. These are USA DODICs: (12ga AA51, AA52, LA51, LA52) (40mm BA06, BA13, BA24, BA25, BA26, BA27), (66 mm FZ15,), (WA97 MCCM nonlethal claymore) LRAD acoustic devices

---

NLW-INST-2502: Advise the unit commander on all aspects of non-lethal weapons and equipment

EVALUATION-CODED: NO   **SUSTAINMENT INTERVAL**: 24 months

DESCRIPTION: The NLW instructor is expected to be able to brief unit commander on all aspects of NLW which include: NLW philosophy, methodologies, implementations strategies, roles and responsibilities, sustainment and integration training, unit NLW readiness and the status of all NLW trained Marines within the unit.

BILLETS: Non-Lethal Weapons Instructor

GRADES: CPL, SGT, SSGT, GYSGT, MSGT, 2NDLT, 1STLT, CAPT

INITIAL TRAINING SETTING: FORMAL

CONDITION: Given a unit and references.

STANDARD: In order to integrate non-lethal weapons/munitions and TTPs into operations.

PERFORMANCE STEPS:
1. Review unit's mission.
2. Review current NL policy.
3. Review current use of force policy.
4. Determine NL training deficiencies.
5. Determine target population description.
6. Develop COA.
7. Brief commander.

REFERENCES:
1. CJCSI 3121.01B Chairman of the Joint Chiefs of Staff Instruction, Standing Rules of Engagement/Standing Rules for the Use of Force for US Forces
2. DODD 3000.3-R Policy for Non-lethal Weapons
3. FM 3-19.15 Civil Disturbance Operations
4. MCO 5500.6F Arming of Law Enforcement and Security Personnel and the Use of Deadly Force
5. MCWP 3-15.8 Multi-service Procedures for the Tactical Employment of Non-lethal Weapons

SUPPORT REQUIREMENTS:

  EQUIPMENT: Marine Corps Escalation of Force Mission Module (EOFMM)

MISCELLANEOUS:

  SPECIAL PERSONNEL CERTS: Interservice non-lethal individual weapons
  instructor course and OC instructor have no expiration date however, TASER
  (HEMI) instructor is valid for 2 years at time of certification.

APPENDIX A

REFERENCES

Field Manual (FM)
FM 3-19.15 Civil Disturbance Operations

Marine Corps Order (MCO)
MCO 5500.6F Arming of Law Enforcement and Security Personnel and the Use of
        Deadly Force

Marine Corps Warfighting Publication (MCWPs)
MCWP 3-15.8 Multi-service Procedures for the Tactical Employment of Non-
        lethal Weapons

Technical Manual
TM 5-4240-536-10 Barrier, Vehicle Arresting, Portable: Vehicle Lightweight
            Arresting Device (VLAD)
TM 9-1377-617-12 Munition, Crowd Control Modular, Nonlethal: M5
TM 9-6350-382-12 Barrier, Vehicle Arresting, Portable (PVAB), M1

Miscellaneous
0000V Rev00 Magnum Spike 2000, Phoenix International
SC0001 Rev00 Sound Commander Operations and Maintenance Manual
MRAD Manual Rev A American Technology Corp Medium Acoustic Device Manual
NLW Manual Controlled F.O.R.C.E. Manual for Mechanical Advantage Control
Holds
Non-lethal MANADNOCK Baton Strike Chart
NLW Force continuum diagram
B.E. Myers GBDIIIC Laser Operator's Manual for GBDIIIC
B.E. Myers 532-M Operator's Manual "Glare" Minigreen Laser System
MARADMIN 560/08 Training and Use of Human Electro-Muscular Incapacitation
(HEMI) Devices
CJCSI 3121.01B Chairman of the Joint Chiefs of Staff Instruction, Standing
Rules of Engagement/Standing Rules for the Use of Force for US Forces
FN 303 OP Manual FN303 Less Lethal Launcher Operator Manual, May 2002
SAT MANUAL Systems Approach to Training Manual
DODD 3000.3-R Policy for Non-lethal Weapons

www.ingramcontent.com/pod-product-compliance
Lightning Source LLC
Chambersburg PA
CBHW080932290526
45795CB00007BA/2716